La Cuisine lyonnaise

Jean ÉTÈVENAUX

Lyonnaise gastronomy

Les Éditions de la Taillanderie

Collection dirigée par Gérald Gambier
Secrétariat de rédaction : Martine Lonvis
Maquette et mise en page : Patricia Brun
Translated into english by : Christopher Kilgallon

COLLECTION «MULTIPLE»

Les cheminées sarrasines. Ghislaine Dulier
Lamartine, poèmes du terroir et du cœur. Emile Magnien
Les grottes d'Azé. Maurice Bonnefoy
Paray-le-Monial. Luc Hopneau (2 langues)
Traboules et miraboules. Louis Jacquemin (4 langues)
Châtillon-sur-Chalaronne. Ouvrage collectif
Les apothicaireries de Bresse et Dombes. Ouvrage collectif
Découverte de Lyon. Louis Jacquemin (6 langues)
Les madones de Lyon. Marie Gouttard
Les moulins du Morvan. Ph. Landry, Ph. Berte-Langereau
Les apothicaireries de Bourgogne. M.T. Girardi
A la rencontre de Guignol. Louis Jacquemin
Faune de Dombes. Yves Thonnérieux
La pêche des étangs. Yves Thonnérieux
La flore des étangs. A.C. Bolomier
Les églises romanes du Forez. Louis Jacquemin
Eglises romanes de Basse-Auvergne. F.P. Fornas
Historial du Saint Curé d'Ars
La pipe de bruyère. Patrick Dubois
Eglises romanes du lyonnais, beaujolais et Viennois. L. Jacquemin
Aqueducs romains de Lyon. J. Etèvenaux
Le Vieux Lyon. L. Jacquemin

© Editions de la Taillanderie - 1996
8, rue du 4 septembre
01009 Bourg-en-Bresse

ISBN 2-87629-161-4
ISSN 1148-5337

Preface

Lyon's culinary art is a most pleasant and often renewed subject for study. Many keen diners from all over the world have had the opportunity to try it, without having recourse to books, with a good deal of application and, more often than not, with a great deal of satisfaction.

The author of this book reminds us that many learned men have surrendered to the charms of Lyon because of its culinary art, and on must admit that, today, the people of Lyon, with great respect for tradition yet with unparalleled culinary inventiveness, and with the help of simple and varied ingredients, share one of their finest assets with the rest of the world.

The specialities of Lyon and its surrounding area : this book lists them marvellously, whether they be internationally famous, like quenelles, Lyon sausage and BEAUJOLAIS wines, or less well known (though unjustly so), like "grattons" (pork scratchings), "matefaim" (thick pancakes) or sabodet (large, boiled pork sausage).

Moreover, the author retraces in a knowledgeable and charming manner, the invention of such dishes, their evolution and, in certain instances, the history or the legend behind them.

Over the years, Lyon has opened itself up to the outside world. So has its culinary art and tradition, to the greater benefit and satisfaction of all. With this gastronomic Vade-mecum, Mr Etèvenaux adds a learned and gourmet contribution to Lyon's international vocation. Lyon gratefully thanks him.

RAYMOND BARRE

DU MÊME AUTEUR

Mademoiselle de Quincié, France-Empire, Paris, 1989, 288 pages

Fouché - Nantes, Nevers, Moulins, Lyon, itinéraires d'un révolutionnaire, La Taillanderie, Bourg-en-Bresse, 1990, 208 pages, Grand Prix de l'Association des auteurs et écrivains lyonnais 1990

Bicentenaire des Éts A. Rey éditeur-imprimeur [partie historique], A. Rey, Lyon, 1991, 160 pages

Les grandes heures de Lyon, Librairie académique Perrin, Paris, 1992, 496 pages + 16 pages hors-texte d'illustrations, Prix du Livre du Conseil général du Rhône 1992

Lyon 1793 - Révolte et écrasement, Horvath, Lyon, 1993, 160 pages, Médaille d'or du Groupe Paris-Lyon 1993

Saint Irénée (IIᵉ siècle) et l'implantation du christianisme, Lugd, Lyon, 1994, 96 pages

Jacquard (1752-1834) et la naissance de l'industrie textile moderne, Lugd, Lyon, 1994, 104 pages

Jean Moulin (1899-1943) et l'organisation de la Résistance, Lugd, Lyon, 1994, 112 pages, Feuille d'Or du Livre sur la place de Nancy 1994

Rabelais (1494-1553) et la naissance de l'humanisme, Lugd, Lyon, 1995, 96 pages

Aqueducs romains de Lyon, La Taillanderie, Bourg-en-Bresse, 1995, 32 pages

édition de : *La France à la conquête du Pacifique - Correspondance de l'élève-officier Achille Amet (1849-1854)*, Osmondes, Paris, 1996, 208 pages

édition de : *Quand Rhône-Alpes faisait la langue française*, Fondation Bullukian, Champagne-au-Mont-d'Or, 1996, 96 pages

en collaboration : *La fresque des Lyonnais*, Les Créations du Pélican, Lyon, 1995, 160 pages

commentaire historique de : Honoré de Balzac, *Le colonel Chabert*, Horvath, Lyon, 1994, 124 pages

The advantages of Lyon's geographical position are obvious with respect to its culinary traditions and habits. As a major cross-roads, Lyon takes advantage of all products coming from the nearby surroundings. The geographical inconvenience of dissimilar and separate regions becomes an advantage both as regards cereal basins as well as pasture land and vineyards on the mountains. This results in an extraordinary variety of produce from the fields and farms even though, in just one century, there has been a constant reduction in the number of livestock as compared with crops and natural vegetation, with agricultural production being substituted for livestock breeding (but dairy products from the Rhone-Alps region are fifth on a national scale).

Nonetheless, the advantages described in 1825 by Anthelme Brillat-Savarin - whose name has since been given to a regional cheese - remain valid even today: «Its position results in an abundance of wines from Bordeaux, Hermitage, Burgundy; the game on the surrounding hillsides is excellent; from the lakes of Geneva and Bourget, one gets the best fish in the world; and connoisseurs swoon at the sight of Bresse fattened pullets for which this city is the central storehouse». *As Félix Benoit was to write later,* «...Lyon's genius for the culinary arts [...] borrows readily from Bresse, Bugey, the Ardèche department, Velay, the Dauphiné and Savoie regions». *It is easy to understand that Paul Bocuse tends to include all the neighbouring regions in greater Lyon...*

Photography
Gérald GAMBIER

Capitale des gueules

The capital of mouth-watering dishes

This rich diversity was highly-appreciated by Stendhal who, as a good citizen of Grenoble, was not, however, among the sycophants of the capital of the Gauls. In 1837, he affirmed; *«I know only one thing which is done well in Lyon; food is prepared in the most excellent of ways there and, in my opinion, better than in Paris. Above all, vegetables are prepared in the most heavenly of manners. [...; the potatoes,] I saw twenty-two different ways to prepare them and at least twelve of these ways are unknown in Paris».* The essential point was thus made concerning the gastronomic dishes prepared using the most ordinary raw materials; this was not to prevent, at the same time, Abel Hugo from claiming in 1835 that most citizens of Lyon *«ate badly, both out of poverty and through frugality».* Chateaubriand painted a more accurate picture when, in 1805, he spoke of a place *«where we are fed so well that I hardly have the courage to leave this splendid city».*

A century later, in 1932, Charles Joanin was to state: *«The family feast - and it really is one, relatively speaking - does not include any sumptuous dishes but only plain produce from the earth, from the livestock, carefully prepared, artistically presented: a soup, hot sausage served the way people from Lyon like it, calf's head, spiced up with a vinaigrette sauce, two boiled chickens, St. George's mushrooms with gravy, roast mutton leg, salad; then the desserts follow the cervelle de canut* bathed in a rich cream and sweet-smelling rigottes (a combined dairy-cow and goat cheese); custard with caramel served with small, crisp dry biscuits and fruits which are in season.»* Foreigners - anyone not from Lyon - discover this highly-valued simplicity upon their arrival, as did the narrator of Calixte, to whom Jean Dufourt proposes in 1926, *«a meal compared with which all those [...] partaken of in Paris or elsewhere would not even deserve a good mark».* In the same period, Sacha Guitry has one of his heroes say: *«Lyon, where one eats so well».*

Then finally, in 1934, Curnonsky - whose real name was Edmond Sailland, but a veritable prince of gastronomes and given to the simple things in life - cried out during a banquet at Vettard's table, the slogan, *«Lyon, capital of gastronomy!»* It is not insignificant that this took place during the Lyon Gastronomy Fair, in which so many men of letters such as Tancrède de Visan - and gastronomes took part. Curnonsky is only repeating the utterances of Léon Daudet, since the famous polemicist had explained: *«Lyon, the capital of French cooking, is crossed, by a third mighty river in addition to the Saône and the Rhone, that of red wine, Beaujolais, which is never murky or dry.»* This is how one becomes the metropolis for gourmets, provided that one never forgets the verity pointed out by Édouard Herriot: *«Guignol's dishes are meals for the poor».*

---

* cervelle de canut = silk weaver's brains, a fresh cheese based preparation with herbs

Gras double

Tripe

For 4 people

Ingredients :
10 dl of wine vinegar
2 decent sized stomachs (tripe butcher)
2 large onions
25 cl of groundnut oil
Salt, pepper.

- Cut the tripe into thin strips.
- Chop the onions.
- Heat up some oil in the frying pan and first add the tripe, then the onions.
- Cook for about 20 minutes, stirring often.
- Add a dash of vinegar just before serving the hot dish.

Les pommes paillasson

Potato mat

For 4 people
500g of potatoes
125g of butter
Salt and ground pepper

- Peel, wash and carefully dry the potatoes. Grate them coarsely then rinse the pulp thus obtained rapidly and press out a maximum of water.
- Spread the pulp out on a thin teacloth, roll it up and squeeze out as much water as you can.
- Melt 40g of butter in a large frying pan. Place the pulp in the frying pan and add salt and pepper.
- Cook the potato mat for about 20 minutes, melting a knob of butter around the edges of the frying pan from time to time.
- Using a wooden spoon, detach the contents of the frying pan and flip it over onto a dish.
- Put another 50 g of butter in the same frying pan. Slide the potato mat back into the frying pan, raw side downwards and continue cooking for another 10 minutes. Serve the dish as soon as its cooked.

Page 9. The tripe made by the Café des Fédérations

Les cardons à la moelle

Cardoons with marrow

For 6 people

Ingredients : 2 large cardoon stalks, 1 lemon, flour,
60g of butter, 150g of beef marrow, 1 bunch of chives, Salt and ground white pepper

- Only use the tender part of the cardoons . Strip off the rib tips.
- Cut the cardoons into even slices then place them in a bowl of water with lemon juice in it.
- Mix the flour into a small quantity of cold water, then pour the mixture into a large saucepan containing 2.5 litres of water. Bring up to the boil, stirring continuously, then add the cardoons.
- Cover the saucepan and leave to cook for 40 minutes at medium heat.
- Strain the cardoons.
- Melt some butter in a frying pan, put the cardoons in the frying pan and stir for about 10 minutes.
- Add salt and pepper.
- Cut the marrow in quite thick slices and poach them for 3 minutes.
- Strain off the water.
- Place the cardoons in a dish, put the pieces of marrow on top of the cardoons. To garnish the dish, sprinkle on a la small quantity of chopped chives.

Salade de groins d'âne aux lardons

Dandelion salad with lardoons

For 4 people

800g of dandelion leaves, 1 clove of garlic, 2 slices of slightly stale country bread
200g of lardoons with the rind removed, Oil, vinegar, salt and pepper

- Wash the dandelions carefully and put them in a salad bowl. Add salt and pepper, then toss the salad.
- Rub the slices of bread with garlic then remove the crust and cut into small cubes.
- Fry the lardoons for 5 minutes in a frying pan with a small quantity of cooking oil.
- Put the lardoons in with the salad and, without first cleaning the frying pan, fry the bread cubes until golden brown. Put these in the salad bowl too.
- Still using the same frying pan, pour in two spoonfuls of vinegar to make a sort of "gravy", and scrape the frying pan with a wooden spatula.
- Pour this onto the salad. Toss the salad again and serve.

Toujours de la cervelle

Brains forever

Lyon meals have their affable side which has always struck observers. On the eve of the Revolution, in 1786, the famous Alexandre-Balthazar Grimod de la Reynière (issuing from a family between Rhone and Saône and who himself had a shop in the rue Mercière displaying exotic products) praised Lyon suppers where *«everyone openly expressed his joy at sharing his repast with others»*; he claimed - a ritual comparison - to prefer them *«to the most brilliant in the Capital»*, pointing out that *«there was a kind of natural ease, graced with social amenities, a feeling of good will, which does not preclude either charms, high spirits, or even epigrams.»* Lyon comes very close to being a metropolis of the spirit! Sixty years later, in 1845, the American D.G. Mitchell noted that the cafés were more heterogeneous than in Paris: *«Here, the proletariat more easily intermingles with the red ribbon of the Legion of Honour, and married working couples may be seen at a table decked with a luxury beer from Strasbourg, whereas at another table, a young trader enjoys a pint of sparkling saint-péray with a military friend»*; at that time, the Lyon institution which was to become the Brasserie Georges had already been in existence for almost ten years and Alsatian breweries had existed since the beginning of the 19th century.

Next to the citizen of Lyon, dull and a bit parsimonious - which is only the bad side of the wish to avoid showing off at any cost - there is a man who appreciates life and who is particularly fond of good living; an author who has written much about his city, Marcel Grancher, has aptly painted the picture of *«a city of hearty drinkers and gourmets, of hume-piots 1 and torche-casseroles 2, of tire-à-boire 3 and of lèche-grils 4.»* The result has been described by Pierre Mérindol: *«An authentic Lyon personage sitting down at the table, this is a veritable feast for the eyes».* Nonetheless, the native is not a man of excesses and he does not like to throw food away, hence the very local art of reusing leftovers. As the politician Justin Godart said, *«there is nothing better than a warmed-over meal»*; in any event, the region abounds with bread soups, French crust and other truffes emmerda (potatoes and eggs mixed together).

At the beginning of the industrialisation period, the emblematic figure of the silk-worker drew attention through his culinary tastes. This is how, in 1841, J. Augier describes him in his Encyclopédie morale du XIXe siècle: *«For breakfast, the silk-worker's food consists of a kind of curd which he mixes with garlic, butter and small onions; for lunch, he eats pickled pork or potatoes with the same curd; for supper, since he sups, he returns a third time to his well-loved cheese, with a bit of fried cod, a fish that he places on par with eels and pike.»* This cheese is, of course, the cervelle de canut and its omnipresence helps one to understand that Paul Bocuse also recommends it as a starter.

La salade d'amourettes

Spinal marrow salad

- Scald the marrow in boiling stock with a touch of salt and vinegar to make them a little firmer.
- sprinkle with parsley blue poppy seeds and cook in a frying pan. When they start to brown, flamber them with whisky.
- Sprinkle onto a bed of green salad leaves.

Restaurant La Bressane
Recipe by Jean-Pierre Duplouy
2, rue de Cuire - 69004 Lyon

Saucisson chaud à la beaujolaise

HOT SAUSAGE - BEAUJOLAIS STYLE

For 6 people
1 raw boiling sausage (800g to 1 kg), 1 bouquet-garni,
100 g of shallots, butter,
Small white onions, mushrooms,
Salt and pepper
1 litre of Beaujolais wine

- Brown the chopped shallots in butter then add the litre of Beaujolais.
- Cook for about 10 minutes
- Add the sausage and the bouquet-garni and continue cooking for another 20 to 25 minutes.
- Remove the sausage and the bouquet-garni.
- Boil the liquid down to about half its volume.
- Skin the sausage cut in into slices (not too thin). Place the slices on a dish.
- Thicken the sauce slightly with a little brown stock or if this is not available, with a small quantity of crushed rusk.
- Gently fry the mushrooms in a little butter, slightly brown the small white onions and ad both to the dish.
- Pour the preparation over the sausage.
- Let the dish cook for a few more minutes the serve with boiled or steamed potatoes sprinkled with a little chopped parsley.

Brasserie Georges
Didier Rinck
Recipe by Marc Grisard
30, cours de Verdun , 69002 Lyon

Page 13. Spinal marrow salad by the Bressane, Croix Rousse and hot sausage Beaujolais style by the Brasserie Georges.

In 1932, Marcel Grancher referred to «*these houses, all in the traditional Lyon style and most of them located near the silk-factory district, where one ate simple but exquisite things, prepared just like at home*». No putting on airs: «*The surroundings were unpretentious. Drink was served in coarse glasses. But what food and what wine!*» And to think «*of Ravier's mutton's foot, Garcin's macaroni gratin, Buisson's tripe, Fage's grilled meats and - especially - Marius Lamour's sole with white wine*». And to mention the mères: Filloux, Brazier - the first woman to be awarded three stars from the Guide Michelin -, Bigot, Pompon, Caron and other Guy's (the latter apparently began in 1759; one should add the most recent ones, that we saw not so long ago, such as the Léa's and the Vittet's. It is impossible to determine the origin of certain chefs of the great families and discover how they were employed after the wars of the 19th century and the beginning of the 20th century. It is not by chance that a great chef such as Christian Bourillot is the grandson of a «*chef of a bourgeois household*».

These women have had a lasting influence on Lyon's culinary traditions, to which they gave its letters patent of nobility without ever denying its folk origins. Paul Bocuse, who nonetheless stems from a family easily going back two hundred years and who has never hidden the pride he takes in repeating their gestures, was to say of mère Brazier: «*This is where I learned to cook simply, which does not mean easily. I learned the necessity of quality products. I learned frugality, but above all, I learned that you cannot succeed without working; this seems mundane to say, but one forgets it all too often.*» So, there doubtless would not be a Monsieur Paul, de Bocuse d'Or - awarded every two years at professional food fairs - and a high-speed train nicknamed Bocuse - so the Americans and the Japanese can enjoy eating out on Sundays - if there had not been the long precedence of several generations, with a special feminine presence.

* N.D.T. 1 dish sniffers 2 pan wipers 3 tipplers and 4 grill lickers

---

La cervelle de canut
Silk weavers brains

For 4 people
2 soft white cheeses, 1 clove of garlic,
15 g of chives, 1 dl of olive oil,
1/2 dl of wine vinegar, 1/2 dl of dry white wine,
Salt and pepper.

- Strain the whey of the cheeses.
- Mix the white cheeses in a dish with the olive oil, the wine vinegar and the white wine.
- Season and mix with a wooden spatula.
- Finely chop the garlic and the chives and mix them together.
- Place the Silk weaver's brains in a bowl.
- Sprinkle with chives and parsley.
- Serve as cold as possible.

Café des Fédérations
Raymond Fulchiron
Recette de Pascal Maninet
8, rue du Major Martin - 69001 Lyon

Page 15. Cervelle de Canut (Silk Weaver's Brains), Café des Fédérations.

Dents de lion et caviar

(dandelions) and caviar

Lyon's vocabulary includes a substantial number of terms referring to local gastronomy. The most well-known are the mâchon, which refers to this second hearty breakfast taken during the morning, comprised of cooked pork meats, cheese and wine, and the bouchon, which refers to the little unpretentious bistrot where one is sure to eat food which is both simple and fortifying, in very friendly surroundings.

These words refer either to specialities or to basic ingredients. Among the former, the bugnes - these fritters, few of which would now conform to the authentic recipe and which, today associated with Mardi Gras, were, at the origin of the first Sunday of Lent, the cervelle de canut - which has definitely taken the place of claqueret, which was a very simple curd -, the gratons - these bits of fried fat which have so long been a favourite of Raymond Barre -, the matefaims - originally thicker than pancakes -, the pogne - a brioche which is found only in the Drome department - and rigottes (a combined dairy-cow and goat cheese) - which now come only from Condrieu and which have not necessarily lost their attractiveness with age.

The other terms have their equivalents in French, but the fact that they are still used locally shows their importance in the preparation of Lyon dishes. We should therefore mention blettes (chards) - whose green leaves are used instead of spinach -, carottes rouges (beets), clapotons (foot of mutton), dents de lion (to be pronounced dents d'lion [dandelion in English] (dandelion leaves), groins d'âne (a variety of the above), caviar du Puy (lentils from Haute-Loire) and truffes (spuds). Others have fallen into disuse; today, one no longer speaks of ballons (currants with mackerels), barboton (mutton stew), cabrillon (small goat cheese), cacoux (eggs), clergeon (tender lettuce), clinquettes (bits of cutlet), doigts-de-mort (salsify, after being peeled), farine jaune (corn flour) gène (pressed marc), manteau (beef undercut), moine (corn salad), oignon de Florence (chives), os de china (pork chops), panure (bread-crumbs whose soft inside part is not necessarily fresh), pelosse (sloe gin), picous (cherry, pear or apple stems) pois gourmand (mange-tout peas), racine jaune (carrot) or petit rave (radishes).

Contrary to what Lyon residents often think, this vocabulary is not their own, and is widely spread over a good part of the Rhone-Alps region, a traditional area where provençal is spoken. They may also have forgotten that certain words are now used throughout France, such as tomme (cheese), and that others deserve to be more widely used, such as rôties - instead of toast, although these slices of bread are not necessarily toasted - which Madame Roland spoke of at the end of the 18th century. And do they know that bacon, in its British sense, belongs to this Rhone-Alps glossary.

Translator's note: please re-see this sentence closely - a bit murky.

Petit salé aux lentilles

Pickled pork with lentils

Recipe for 8 people:
3 kilog of salted top ribs
2 sabodets (speciality sausages)
3 carrots
2 onions
1 bouquet-garni (thyme, laurel)
500 g of green lentils

- Cook the pickled pork and the two sabodets in simmering non-salted water, with a carrot and an onion - - Leave the sabodet 30 minutes, the pickled pork 2 hours to 2 1/2 hours.
- Put butter, two carrots and a finely diced onion in a saucepan; warm gently without frying,
- Add the lentils and the bouquet-garni, add water to 3 cm above the ingredients, allow to cook without boiling and without salting.
- Just before the end of cooking, remove the bouquet-garni, salt lightly, pepper, add the top ribs, the sabodets, finish cooking.
- Serve very hot with chopped parsley on top.

Brasserie Le Nord
Recipe by Frédéric Berthod
18, rue Neuve - 69002 Lyon

Salade de lentilles

Lentil salad

For 4 people : 350 g of lentils, 1 clove of garlic, 2 onions, 25 g of butter, 1 bouquet-garni, 50 cl of white wine, olive oil, sherry vinegar, Dijon mustard, parsley (flat leafed variety), salt, pepper

- Soak the lentils in luke-warm water for 1 hour.
- Strain the lentils. Melt the butter in a stewpan.
- Add the garlic chopped in two and the finely diced onions, then the bouquet-garni. Stir for 2 to 3 minutes.
- Add the lentils and stir all ingredients together.
- Add the white wine, top up with a large glass of water and bring to the boil. Turn the burner to low position and leave to cook for about 40 minutes.
- Prepare a vinaigrette sauce composed of 6 soup spoons of olive oil, 2 soup spoons of vinegar and 1 soup spoonful of mustard, plus salt and pepper.
- Beat the ingredients together to obtain a smooth mixture.
- Strain the lentils and pour into a salad bowl.
- Remove the bouquet-garni.
- Before serving, pour on the vinaigrette and decorate with chopped parsley.

Page 17. Pickled pork with lentils, the Restaurant du Nord.

Doux jésus

Sausages are doubtless what comes most quickly to mind when typifying Lyon. However, distinctions should be made by taking a close look at the jésus (wrapped up in a net such as Enfant-Jésus and rather like a plump, pretty little baby), the rosette (a sliced sausage, made in the rectum of a pig's entrails, whose anus is said to resemble a small rose), the saveloy (with pistachios or truffles, but without brains), the sabodet (raw, with pig's head and rind), and hot sausages (to be served, like the saveloy, with steamed potatoes and butter) and baked like a brioche (in the past, one said: en brioche). As for the Lyon sausage itself, it is comprised of lean ham pounded with a mortar with narrow strips of bacon, giving it a bright, streaked appearance; pork butchers quite sometimes simply call it raw sausage.

In any case, this is the most refined example of Lyon's predilection for cooked pork meats - and seems to date back to the Gallo-Roman period. This comes first from a necessity: to secure meat which was not too dear; put otherwise, always simple, down-to-earth cooking. But, as they are inventive, Lyon residents used pork in all possible ways, from simple pig's feet and tails with tripe, including rolls of rind and *rolled head* (a sort of galantine which also includes pig and beef tongue); there is also blood-sausage, highly appreciated by anticlerical individuals if it comes from Crépieux-la-Pape, since they enjoy it particularly on Holy Friday, under the name of the Pope's blood sausage.

Another confusion to be avoided, Lyon andouillette is made using only calf's ruffle, although Édouard Herriot used to say that, "as with politics, it always smells a little bit like dung - an allusion to pig entrails used at that time. In the same way, the tablier du sapeur (whose name was invented by the Maréchal de Castellane, the military governor of Lyon under Napoleon III), is taken from calf's ruffle in a mixture of eggs and breadcrumbs. But, connoisseurs of real sausage must be careful: Marcel Grancher points out that for Grasalard, the only ones which were really good were *«those sausages, with black spots, the old Bugey or Dauphiné type»*; it was necessary for these cayons to have been fed *«ground barley, broad beans, chestnuts, acorns, corn flour and oats...»*.

Page 20. Andouillettes and pork scratchings, Colette Sibilla at the Halles de Lyon.

Andouillettes au vin blanc sec

Andouillettes in dry white wine.

- Place the andouillettes in an oven dish.
- Pour in the white wine to half cover the andouillettes.
- Add a few knobs of butter.
- Cook in the oven for 1 hour.
- Turn the andouillettes over now and again so that they brown on both sides.

Jean-Pierre Dheyriat - L'Andouillette Châtillonnaise Châtillon-sur-Chalaronne

Les paquets de couennes

Pork rind bundles

For 4 people
5 or 6 strips of pork rind
2 onions
2 cloves
2 carrots
1 litre of chicken stock
Lard
1 bunch of parsley (flat-leafed variety)
Salt and pepper.

- Cut the pork rind into short pieces and group the pieces in bundles of 5 or 6 and tie them up with string.
- Peel the onions and stick a clove into each of them.
- Peel and finely chop the carrots.
- Place the rind bundles, the clove-spiked onions and the carrots in a stewpan.
- Cover the ingredients with the chicken stock and bring to the boil.
- Leave to cook for two and a half hours.
- After cooking, strain the liquid off the rind bundles.
- Put some lard in a large frying pan, heat it up and place the rind bundles in it.
- Brown the rind bundles with salt and pepper.
- Chop the parsley and add it to the rind bundles.
- Stir the dish and serve.

Page 21. With truffles, pistachios or just plain...succulent boiling sausages by Colette Sibilla at the Halles de Lyon, Cours Lafayette.

Que d'eau, que d'eau !

Water! water!

Water is not merely the force which has supplied electric power and provided better irrigation for the Rhone national countryside; it is also the place where crayfish (Nantua lake), carp (Dombes), pike (Ain) and trout (Rhone and Alpine tributaries) thrive, along with all the other similar small fried fish from the Saône. Salt-water fish too are welcome on the tables of Lyon citizens, whether this involves mullet, bass, mackerel, angler-fish, salmon, sea bream, sole, dab, sainte-pierre, whiting, cod or herring (very highly-appreciated as a starter with cold potatoes and called gendarme in the past); seafood is so highly appreciated that a great restaurant such as Bourillot uses one ton of mussels per season.

The importance of fish had been noted as early as 1783 by Berthelet de Barbot in his *Topographie médicale de Lyon et de son territoire*. Moreover, he found Rhone fish *«preferable»* over those from the Saône, reserving his highest praise for fish from Lake Leman and the Ain department, but ever wary of fish from ponds in the Dombes - which he included in Bresse. He also noticed all fish which came from the *«two seas»*, even though they could, *«in warm weather [...] rot due to their being removed far away from where they were caught»*. Their high consumption was also linked to the practice of meatless meals at Lent and every Friday.

Rice is served with certain fish, as are quenelles. The latter, it should be remembered, are also linked to the production of water, since, if we are to believe Mathieu Varille, they are made quite simply of *«one-third fish, preferably pike, one-third beef marrow or calf kidney fat and one-third chou paste»* (in fact, there are quite different recipes: Jean Ducloux, in his Greuze restaurant, assigns one-half to fish and Christina Bourillot sometimes goes even further). In spite of certain purists, they can also be prepared in vol-au-vent or in gratin.

The presence of water is also responsible for numerous truck-farms of which one still sees traces both in Pierre-Bénite's restaurant (famous for his salads) as well as around Vaulx-en-Velin and Décines (whose melons were famous). There has always been a constant demand for garlic and onions - which are even prepared stuffed.

Marinière d'anguilles en matelote

Eels stewed in wine sauce

For 4 people
800 g of dressed and sliced eel sections
1.5 litres of fish concentrate with red wine
1.5 litres of red wine, shallots
12 Paris mushroom heads
12 onion tops
12 cherry tomatoes
Butter - 4 sandwich-loaf bread croutons
100 g of scalded lardoons

- Poach the eels in the concentrate for 7 to 8 minutes. After cooking, remove the central bone, put aside for later use .
- Boil down one-half litre of red wine and shallots, reduce the concentrate and cook for 30 minutes, remove the fat.
- Slightly thicken the sauce, reduce, run through strainer, thicken with butter.
- Cook the garnish, onion tops, mushrooms, tomatoes.
- Dress the eel pieces in the dish, separate with vegetables, coat with sauce, add a crouton on the side.

Restaurant Larivoire
Recette de Bernard Constantin
Chemin des Iles
69140 Rillieux-la-Pape

Raie au beurre noisette

Butterball Skate

For 4 people
1kg 200 g of thick skate (preferably a thornback)
200 g of butter
10 cl of red wine vinegar
Parsley, carrot, salt, pepper

- Cut the skate into 4 pieces, then poach it in a court-bouillon to which about 5cl of peanut oil has been added.
- Remove the two skins (the black one and the white one).
- Make the butterballs with fresh parsley and capers.
- Serve with steamed potatoes.

Restaurant Le Pasteur
Recipe by Louis Chabanel
83 quai Perrache
Lyon (2nd district)

Page 25. Eels stewed in wine sauce, la Rivoire at Rillieux-la-Pape.

Carpe royale de Dombes farcie au coeur de cardons

Royal carp from the Dombes
stuffed with cardoon heart

For 4 people: One 1.5 kilogram carp
Preparation for reducing the white wine:
75 centilitres of Saint-Véran - 3 large white onions - 1 head of garlic cut in two, horizontally - 200 g of celery in sticks - 1 decilitre of fine cooking oil - salt and pepper.

— Heat the oil; scald the onions, garlic and branch celery. Use a spatula to mix over brisk heat for five minutes. Add the wine, wait until it comes to a boil, then flambé it and reduce the volume by one-third and add one-half litre of water. Reduce again by half, salt, pepper and run through the strainer.
-Scale the carp, trim it, remove the centre bone by the back of the fish then gut it, place it in an oval dish, salt and pepper.

For the stuffing:
4 slices of farmhouse bread - 20 g of butter - fine salt - coarse salt - pepper - 50 g of flour - 2 lemons - 1 kilogram of cardoons - 100 g of fresh morels - 2 egg yolks.
— Cut the first cardoon branches in order to make a normal bone-marrow gratin and keep only 200 g of tender, soft heart.
Use a knife to peel and taper the vegetable, from top to bottom.
To cook the Cardoons:
— Prepare the white wine based "blanc" ": place a strainer over a saucepan, sift 50 g of flour, add 2 litres of cold water, a handful of coarse salt and 2 lemons, cut in half.
— Cut the cardoons in thin strips. Cook the cardoons in this "blanc" for 40 minutes then drain and pour them into a salad bowl.
— Dice the bread and brown it in butter in a frying pan, then drain and add to the cardoons. Cut the morels in half and braise them and add to the previous preparation. Mix together. Allow to cool; season to taste and add the egg yolks.
— Fill the carp with this stuffing then tie it up it like a "roast".
— Turn on the oven, thermostat 8 (250°). Pour the sauce around the carp in an oval dish; cook the carp for 15 minutes on each side, sprinkling it every 15 minutes.
Once it is cooked, allow to settle 5 minutes, serve in a serving dish. Pour its juice through the strainer into a saucepan; thicken with 40 g of butter. Cut the string, remove the skin, coat with sauce. Serve the dish to the guests and taste it; serve it with a Pouilly-Fuissé "Château de Beauregard" or a Saint-Véran J. Saumaize.

Restaurant l'Alexandrin
Recipe by Alain Alexanian
Lyon (3rd district)

Page 27. Stuffed carp with cardoons, l'Alexandrin.

Gratin de queues d'écrevisses

Crayfish tail gratin

Ingredients for 1 portion :
20 crayfish, crayfish butter, cream, salt, pepper.
- Cook the crayfish in boiling water for 5 minutes.

- Detach the tails and brown them in a frying pan with a teaspoonful of crayfish butter.
- Peel the tails.
- Start the sauce by adding the cognac. Add the cream (1 scoop) and boil down.
- Add salt and pepper.
One can add a hollandaise sauce, brown under a slow grill, and decorate with flaky pastries.

Les trois saucissons de Coco

«Mon amie Colette Sibilia»

Coco's three sausages
"My friend Colette Sibilia"

Take three sorts of sausage :
- *ordinary,*
- *with truffles,*
- *with pistachios*

- Place them in cold water and bring to the boil gently. Let them cook for about 40 minutes.
- Put some potatoes to cook in the same water
- When the potatoes are cooked, the sausages will be too.
- Take 200 g of butter. Melt it. Add pistachios and crumbs of truffle.
- Cut the sausages into slices and pour the melted butter mixture onto them and the potatoes.

Restaurant Le Pasteur
Recipe by Louis Chabanel
83 quai Perrache
Lyon (2nd district)

28

Page 29. Pike quenelle, Café des Fédérations.

Quenelle de brochet

Pike quenelle

For 4 people
4 pike quenelles (about 120 g each)
800 g of lobster soup
30 cl of cream
Brandy
Salt and pepper

- Mix the cream with the lobster soup.
- Add a dash of brandy and bring to the boil.
- Pour the sauce into a dish and place the quenelles in it (the sauce should cover the quenelles to about 3/4).
- Bring back up to the boil then put in the oven (160° - 170°C) for about 20 minutes.
- Serve hot straight from the oven.

Café des Fédérations
Raymond Fulchiron
Recette de Pascal Maninet
8, rue du Major Martin - 69001 Lyon

Page 30. Quenelles by Colette Sibilla at the Halles de Lyon.

Demi-deuil pour Carême

Demi-deuil for Lent

Although the region has long been occupied by man, Lyon and Rhone Alps citizens have always paid their respects to nature and its other inhabitants. Even today, hunting is highly developed and wild game and fowl complete the ordinary fare from farmyards, ponds and meadows. Bresse poultry go very nicely with crayfish and Nantua sauce, whereas pike from the Dombes add a lovely scent to quenelles from Bourg-en-Bresse and Lyon. And as not all the birds have not taken refuge in the Villars-les-Dombes ornithology park, mallards are also often served.

Next to the sumptuous poularde (fattened chicken) demi-deuil (the Lent chef had invented a variety of them for the Lyon Maréchal Suchet, and were referred to, from his ducal title as à la d'Albufera) or in bladder, chicken with vinegar (and white wine) remains a simple, tasty dish. The one with cream comes from Bresse and requires egg yolks. Sautéed with crayfish, it is a part of Dauphinois culinary traditions.

In the tradition of simplicity, we note the regional taste for poultry giblets (in the Middle Ages, one also ate gizzard salads). Some, in stews, provide the filling. Others - such as liver - are used in the preparation of succulent gratins, that are called cakes, and which, whether or not served with quenelles, go nicely with a tomato sauce, green olives (which are produced not far away, in the Drome department), and mushrooms. They may also be used for stuffing, used both in salads as well as sauces, quenelles as well as Savoie cakes.

With respect to meat, this often continues to come from the Charolais, famous for its succulent beef and sheep (moreover, the race is also bred near Lyon); the lamb nursed by the ewe is also highly-appreciated. It may be served with small game, such as fillet of beef with woodcock. Sirloins of beef, fricassees, escalopes, roasts, fillets and saddles should not make one forget the veal knuckles / ham hocks of calf, kidneys, stews and other pot-au-feu. Calf's liver, although not especially appreciated by the younger generations, may be served in many ways.

One should also speak of ducks, turkeys - that are sometimes called Crémieu skylarks -, pigeons, rabbits, hares, young boars, roebucks - like the gigot à la Beaujeu - and of everything around Lyon! One of these cooked fowls inspired Gabriel Chevallier to create a lovely proverb: *«When one always eats truffled turkey, one ends up treating it like ordinary boiled meat»*.

Page 32-33. Poulard «Demi-Deuil» by the «Mère» Brazier.

Volaille demi-deuil

Chicken "Demi-Deuil" (half-mourning).

For 4 people
A 1.8 kg Bresse chicken (plucked and drawn)
1 small truffle. A few carrots.
1 bunch of leaks, a few small turnips, a muslin or gauze cloth, mustard, pickled morello
cherries, coarse sea salt.

- Cut the truffle into four slices. Slip the slices of truffle under the skin of the chicken
filets and drumsticks.
- Wrap the chicken in a tightly drawn muslin cloth. Tie it up with string under the
wings and drumsticks to hold them in place. Put the carrots, the leaks and the turnips in
a stewpan. Add a little salt. Fill half way up with water. Bring to the boil. Place the
chicken in the stewpan once the contents are boiling. The liquid should just cover the
chicken. Leave to cook at a gentle heat for 3/4 of an
hour.
- Serve accompanied with morello cherries and coarse
grained salt.
- We serve this dish with rice cooked in the chicken
stock.

Restaurant la Mère Brazier
Jacotte Brazier
Recette de Sylvain Gonnet
12, rue Royale - 69001

Poulet au vinaigre

Chicken in vinegar

For 4 people
One 1.4 kilogram farm-chicken, cut up into 4 parts, 1 teaspoon of oil, 2 chopped clove of
garlic, 1 nice onion, pealed and diced, 2 chopped shallots, 4 tomatoes, 1 soupspoon of
tomato concentrate, 25 centilitres of wine vinegar, 30 centilitres of dry white wine, 12.5°,
50 centilitres of thin cream, 2 branches of tarragon and thyme, 10 centilitres of veal
gravy, Salt, pepper

Preparation 30 minutes, cooking, around 45 minutes
- Render and lightly scorch brown the pieces of chicken in oil along with the giblets in
a frying pan
- Remove the pieces of chicken and add garlic, onion and shallots in the frying pan,
allow to render for a few minutes without browning. -
Add the tomatoes, flour, the tomato concentrate.
- Mix, add the vinegar, the white wine, the veal
gravy, tarragon, thyme, salt, pepper.

Hugon bouchon lyonnais
Recette d' Arlette Hugon
12, rue Pizay - 69001 Lyon

Page 35. Chicken in vinegar,
«Bouchon» «Chez Hugon».

Les fraises de veau

Calf's ruffle

- Scald the calf's ruffle for 10 minutes in slightly salted and vinegar laced stock.
- Cook in a frying pan along with some onions and blanched tomatoes.
- Add a few tomatoes towards the end of cooking time, since the first ones added will have "melted down". Sprinkle with blue poppy seeds, salt, pepper and allspice.
- When the preparation starts to brown, flamber it

Restaurant La Bressane
Recipe by Jean-Pierre Duplouy
2, rue de Cuire - 69004 Lyon

Tendron de veau

Veal tendron Hugon style

For 6 people
6 Veal tendrons
2 onions, 4 cloves of garlic, 3 shallots
10 g of oil
50 g of flour
Veal gravy
Thyme
1 litre of dry white wine
6 fresh tomatoes
1 spoonful of tomato concentrate
salt, pepper,
1 litre of thin cream

- Scorch the cubes of veal in very little oil, then put them aside in a casserole.
- Brown the onions, garlic, shallots, tomatoes, tomato concentrate in the frying pan; then sprinkle with flour
- Thicken the veal gravy with white wine, salt, pepper. Add the thyme. Pour the mixture into the casserole, cook for around 1 and a half hours over a low fire.
- After cooking, remove the pieces, reduce the sauce with the thin cream for around 1 hour.
- Run the sauce through the strainer and season to taste.
- Serve with fresh pasta.

Hugon bouchon lyonnais
Recette d' Arlette Hugon
12, rue Pizay - 69001 Lyon

Page 37. Calf's ruffle, restaurant La Bressane.

Tête de veau à la truffe noire du Périgord, consommé aux petits légumes nouveaux

Calf's head with black Périgord truffles, consommé with early spring vegetables

For 5 people
1 calf's head (preferably purchased from a real tripe butcher).
3 litres of chicken stock., 1 carrot, 1 onion, 1 bouquet garni, 1 leak

Trimmings :
1 bunch of carrots tops - a few fresh beans, 1 bunch of turnip tops
2 bunches of spring onions, 2 bunches of wild asparagus
1 bunch of dwarf fennel, 1 bunch of spring leaks
2 bunches of small violet artichokes, 100g of truffles (Tuber melanosporum)
5 cl of truffle juice.

Consommé
700g of lean minced beef
1 onion, 1 carrot, parsley stalks
4 egg whites

-(1) Cook the calf's head in the chicken stock along with the trimmings for about 2 hours.
- Remove the calf's head and strain of the stock. Leave to cool.
- Mix the ingredients for the consommé : lean minced beef, onions, carrot, parsley stalks (dice these ingredients) and the egg whites.
- Mix this with the cold chicken stock.
- Cook again gently for about 3 hours.
- The consommé will settle and clarify during cooking.
- Remove the calf's head, filter the stock, cook all the vegetables in the chicken stock and go back and repeat step (1).
- Strain the consommé through a muslin cloth. Season to taste.
- Add the truffle juice and the finely sliced truffles.
- Serve the calf's head and the vegetables hot.

Restaurant Le Passage
Recipe by Christian Bacque
8, rue du Plâtre - 69001 Lyon

Page 39. Calf's head, restaurant «Le Passage».

Gâteau de foies de volaille

Poultry liver cake "Hugon" style

For 6 people
450 g of white poultry liver, 4 slices of bread, 4 whole eggs, 4 cloves of garlic + parsley, 1/2 litre of milk, Pike quenelle garnish, salt, pepper, 50 g of flour and 50 g of butter

- Chop up the liver, parsley and garlic
- Make a béchamel, include 4 egg yolks, the bread that you have previously dipped in milk and then dried, the chopped up liver, parsley, garlic, salt, pepper
- Beat the egg whites and pour them carefully into the mixture
- Pour everything into a buttered mould. Allow to bake in the double-saucepan for 35 minutes with a medium oven.
- The liver cake can be served with a creamed sauce (béchamel or Nantua).

Hugon bouchon lyonnais
Recette d' Arlette Hugon
12, rue Pizay - 69001 Lyon

Volaille en vessie

Poulard "en vessie"

For 6 people : *1 Bresse poulard (fattened pullet), 1 pigs bladder, vinegar, 300g of fine pork sausage meat, 1 sprig of parsley, 1/2 of a truffle, 100 g of goose liver paté, 1 egg, 2 small glasses of brandy, coarse salt, 1 small glass of Madeira, 2 litres of chicken stock, fine grained salt, pepper*

- Soak the bladder overnight with a mixture of coarse grained salt and vinegar. The next morning, rinse it thoroughly and dry it.
- Soak the poultry for 4 hours in ice cold water so that it stays perfectly white.
- Mix together the sausage meat, the poulard's liver diced into small pieces, the chopped parsley, the finely chopped truffle and the goose liver paté (broken into small pieces), then add the egg as a binder an a small glass of brandy. Ass salt and pepper.
- Put this stuffing inside the poulard then truss it.
- Place the poulard inside the pigs bladder with two large pinches of coarse grained salt, some pepper, a glass of Madeira and a glass of cognac. With a needle, prick the poulard so that it won't split, then hermetically seal the bladder with tightly drawn knots. Pour the stock into a stewpan and bring it up to the boil, then place the poulard in the stock and leave it to poach for about an hour and a half.
- Cut the bladder open just before serving the dish.

Page 41, Liver cake, «Bouchon» «Chez Hugon».

Poulet de Bresse à la crème

Bresse chicken in cream

- Cut the chicken into 8 portions. Brown them in butter in a large cast iron saucepan on a hot gas ring. Add salt and pepper.
- Add the white brandy and flamber. Brown again for a short while. Pour in the white wine so as to half cover the chicken portions. Put the lid on the saucepan. Leave to cook for 40 to 50 minutes depending on the size of the chicken portions. remove the portions of chicken and place them in warm storage.
- Add white wine to the gravy and bring back to the boil to reduce the acidity of the wine. Boil of some of the liquid.
- Add the cream. Boil again to thicken and add an egg yolk to bind the sauce. Pour the sauce over the chicken portions.

Blanquette de Veau

Veal blanquette "Hugon" style

1.8 kilog of veal (veal with bone, top part of cutlets, tendron or shoulder).
3 onions, 4 cloves of garlic
1 white part of leek
1 bunch of herbs
1 litre of dry white wine 12.5°
one-half litre of thin cream
1 lemon
Butter, oil, salt, pepper
Veal stock

- Brown the pieces of meat in a half-butter and half-oil mixture.
- Add the onions, garlic, sprinkle with flour. Mix thoroughly for a few minutes. Add the dry white wine and the water and the thyme, then the leek, the salt, pepper, veal stock. Allow to simmer for around 90 minutes
- Remove the pieces of meat. Reduce the sauce with the half-slice of lemon and the thin cream.
- Run the sauce through the strainer, add a handful of capers.
- Serve everything with rice or fresh pasta.

Hugon bouchon lyonnais
Recette d' Arlette Hugon
12, rue Pizay - 69001 Lyon

Page 43. Veal blanquette, «Bouchon» Chez Hugon and Chicken in cream, Bresse

Pages 44-45. The famous pigs and the three hot sausages, Loulou Chabanel, au «Pasteur».

Gratins des Alpes

Alp Gratins

Gratin exists in various forms. The simplest is made of vegetables, such as squash (in Lyon, this word refers to all sorts of gourd-type plants, also good for soups) or cardoons (an example, in fact, of the «false» vegetable of poor people). There is the version with potatoes, or, more precisely, several versions, according to which one differentiates gratin Dauphinois - only with milk - from savoyard - with cream, sometimes with bacon and which is apparently much older - and from bugiste - with cheese. Having become so famous as to be present in preserves all over France or to have eggs and nutmeg added to it, it is no longer very common in Lyon but even so, rather widely-spread (even more so in private homes than in restaurants).

On the menu in restaurants preparing Lyon-style dishes, macaroni gratin comes from the other side of the Alps. Doubtless very old ties with Italy had favoured its adaptation (it was already being served before the Revolution). Moreover, it is based on an old regional tradition for making pastry, which underwent its last great popular development during the Second World War when it became a necessity. More recently, the appearance of Royans raviole provided a Rhone-Alps variety to Italian traditions. This is doubtless not foreign to the pastry industry, with manufacturers such as Lustucru in Grenoble and Rivoire and Carret in Lyon in the past - today replaced by Panzani.

As in the rest of France, starchy foods are declining in everyday meals, in favour of fresh products and pre-cooked dishes. But potatoes are being rejuvenated with paillasson potatoes (different sorts of girdle cakes cooked slowly in the frying pan and that Alain Chapel sprinkled with fines herbs); on the other hand, salads of cold noodles seem to be a thing of the past.

Finally, how can one not mention seafood gratins, specially those made with crayfish tails, with cream - more exactly, a creamy béchamel with crayfish butter - served very hot, they are unforgettable. The authentic ones, with a few mushrooms and morsels of truffles, are called à la Nantua.

Page 46. Crayfish «au gratin»
Bugey style and cream of pump-
kin soup, Bresse style.

Le tablier de sapeur

Sapper's apron

- Buy a honeycomb stomach at the tripe butcher's.
- Cut it into portions of about 200g.
- Steep for 2 days in a mixture of white wine, vinegar, pepper and salt.
- Boil the marinade.
- Add cream.
- Strain the "aprons" then coat them with egg and bread crumbs.
- Cook for 5 to 8 minutes in a frying pan in a mixture of butter and cooking oil until golden-brown.
- Serve with a hot chive sauce on a very hot plate.

Le Bouchon " Chez Marcelle"
Recipe by Marcelle Bramy
71, Cours Vitton, Lyon (6th district).

Foie de veau

Calf's liver

- Buy some nice pieces of suckling calf's liver (liver of an animal not old enough to graze).
- Cook in butter to taste (rare, medium, well done).
- Place the liver on a hot plate and sprinkle
with chopped parsley.
- Add a little vinegar to the butter to make
"gravy" and pour over the liver and parsley.
- Serve with steamed potatoes.

Le Bouchon " Chez Marcelle"
Recipe by Marcelle Bramy
71, Cours Vitton, Lyon (6th district).

Page 49. The famous calf's liver and Sappers Aprons bny the great Marcelle.

Trompettes-de-la-mort

(craterellus mushrooms)

As a region where vast spaces are not lacking and where people like to go looking for natural products on their own, the Rhone-Alps has many varieties of mushrooms. One does not care much for cultivated mushrooms, not only because they are from Paris, but also because they have no odour and are tasteless in relation to mushrooms picked in meadows and woods. In any event, at the beginning of the century, the père Filloux - the husband of the woman who was the original *«mère»* of Lyon culinary delights, famous especially for her artichoke bottoms with goose liver with truffles, spent her time peeling mushrooms.

The St. George's mushroom - which has become very rare - is seen more and more frequently in the preparation of different dishes, doubtless because it is eaten with juice from meat, browned in the frying pan. But there are also petits roses, sainte-georges and boules de neige, or even puff-balls. Boletus mushrooms are highly sought after. More difficult to find, chanterelles - or girolles - and other trompettes-de-la-mort make the mouths of mushroom connoisseurs water. Morels continue to appeal to the taste buds but unfortunately, truffles no longer come from Valromey, even if Paul Bocuse made his fame with his soup dedicated to Valerie Giscard d'Estaing, when the latter was President of France (in fact, this involves a chicken broth with small vegetables and fresh truffles whose bouquet encompasses the diner when he bites into the flaky pastry crust.

It would be difficult to overestimate the importance of lettuce - which is always eaten after the main dish. Originally, it came not only from truck-farmers, scattered around the entire conglomeration, but above all, from the fields. On Sundays, families go on outings to pick dandelion leaves (the famous dents-de-lion). Lamb's lettuce (which used to be called poule grasse), cardamine (under the vines) and other corn salads vary the pleasures obtained from eating leafy vegetables . These salads are also sometimes to be found in «mixed» varieties, and in this case, are eaten as starters. Small hot lardons, herrings, soft-boiled eggs or poultry gizzards are added, according to individual tastes (with or without toasted croutons and «red» carrots).

Page 50. Artichokes with liver
paté, the «Mère» Brazier.

Fond d'artichaut au foie gras

Artichoke hearts with poultry liver paté

For 4 people
4 large artichokes
300g of mixed, washed salad (scarola, batavia, lolarossa, etc...)
4 generous slices of poultry liver paté (either duck or goose).
Vinaigrette : mustard, vinegar, oil, salt and pepper.

- Pull the stalks off the artichokes (don't cut them). Push the blade of a small, sharp knife into the artichoke to the depth of the bristles and in the centre of the bottom. Use a circular cutting motion. Remove the side leaves. Place in cold water and bring to the boil. Leave to cook for 15 minutes.
- The hearts are cooked when you can pierce them easily with a fork. Leave them in the water they were cooked in.
- Make a breakfast bowlful of vinaigrette. Use some of this on the salad. Put the artichoke hearts in the rest of the vinaigrette.
- Place the salad on a plate. Place an artichoke heart on the salad (shake off excess vinaigrette first).
- Place the slice of liver paté on top.
- We serve this dish with hot toast

Restaurant la Mère Brazier
Jacotte Brazier
Recette de Sylvain Gonnet
12, rue Royale - 69001

La sauce lyonnaise

Lyonnaise sauce

For 50 cl of sauce :
4 onions
50g of butter
20 cl of vinegar
20 cl of white wine
40 cl of beef stock
1 soup spoonful of tomato concentrate
Salt and pepper

- Peel and chop the onions
- Melt the butter in a saucepan and add the onions. Cook them until they turn light brown.
- When they are almost cooked, add the vinegar and the wine.
- Let the liquid boil off until there is about the volume of a half a glass left in the bottom of the saucepan.
- Add the beef stock and the tomato concentrate and leave to simmer for another ten minutes.

Odeurs de sainteté

Odours of saintliness

Although one must be careful not to reduce Lyon's gastronomy to a single one of its ingredients, one must note the exceptional variety of the cheese board. It is very symbolic of the geographical position of this cross-roads region. Blue cheeses also come not only from Morbier, Gex and Bresse but from Montbrison and Ambert. Hard cheese comes from Savoie as well as from Auvergne. Picodons and rigottes are to be found on both sides of the Rhone. The mountains also supply both beaufort and reblochon (the largest cheese production in the region: 10 000 tons per year) as well as cantal and comté, whereas the Beaujolais hillsides provide boutons de coulotte and the banks of the impetuous waters provide the caillous du Rhone. Pleasant mixtures are used to add scents to marc. The art of seasoning leftovers extends even to the strong cheese of Beaujolais (with or without marc), the cheese à la lyonnaise (including leak bouillon), the Croix-Rousse cheese (blue cheese and goat cheese mixed with white wine and steeped for several weeks) and the Franch-Comté cream-cheese. The crowning glories of these cheeses are the saint-marcellin, saint-félicien and, from the Auvergne puys, saint-nectaire - not to forget tamié and chambarand prepared in Alpine abbeys bearing these names.

In a word, coming from monts d'Or or the Dauphiné, the Mâconnais region or the Ardèche, they are numerous and highly cherished. Whenever people from Lyon get together to eat simply - even if only for a buffet - it is unthinkable for there not to be cheese (which may also come from other places, as does brie). They constitute the natural complement to cooked pork meats served as starters. One drinks not only red wine with them, but white wine as well (the latter goes very well with goat cheese).

These cheeses are also used in numerous dishes, from Lyon onion soup au gratin and Savoie soup (prepared simply or à la Bocuse) up through tarts, covered tarts and quiches, not to mention ravioles or the fondu; more recently, one has seen mixtures of curd and fruit. In a more sophisticated but nonetheless more traditional way, grated and gratiné emmenthal on rays is most pleasant to the pallet.

How could one forget that a citizen of the Rhone-Alps - Brillat-Savarin - was to say that *«a meal without cheese is like a beautiful girl with one eye»*?

Gratinée à l'oignon

Onion soup "au gratin"

For 8 people
200g of onions, 50g of butter, 75g of gruyere cheese, 50g of flour, 1 clove of garlic, 5 egg yolks, 1/2 litre of white wine, 1 1/2 litres of consommé, 1 glass of Madeira.

- Gently brown the finely chopped onions in a saucepan with the butter and the clove of garlic.
- When they are lightly browned, add the flour.
- Brown them a little more then add the white wine, the consommé or, if the latter is not available, with the same quantity of water.
- Add salt and pepper and leave to cook for 15 minutes.
- Cut some thin slices of bread.
- Toast them lightly in the oven or under the grill.
- Pour the soup into a soup dish (oven proof).
- Float the slices of toast on the surface of the soup.
- Sprinkle with grated gruyere cheese.
- Place in the oven and leave to cook "au gratin".
- Remove from the oven and add the egg yolks and the glass of Madeira. Serve very hot.

Brasserie Georges
Didier Rinck
Recipe by Marc Grisard
30, cours de Verdun
69002 Lyon

Tripes gratinées

Tripe "au gratin"

3 carrots, 2 onions, 1/2 litre of white wine, 2.5 kg of second stomach, 1 spoonful of tomato concentrate, 2 spoonfuls of flour, 1 kg of tomatoes, 1l of veal stock

- Brown the carrots and the chopped onions in a little butter.
- Add the flour and tomato concentrate, then start the sauce by adding the white wine.
- Add a little crushed fresh tomato, the veal stock and the pieces of tripe which should have been previously marinated in a little white wine with some mixed herbs.
- Add a clove, some bay leaves, salt and pepper and leave to stew for a day.
- Put the tripe in an earthenware oven dish.
- Add sliced potatoes, sprinkle lightly with gruyere cheese or bread crumbs according to taste.
- Serve and enjoy !

Au petit bouchon Chez Georges
Recipe by France Deschamps
8, rue des Garets - 69001 Lyon

Page 55. Tripe from the «Bouchon» Chez Georges and a gratinée from the Brasserie Georges.

Guignol et gratte-cul

Guignol and rose hips

The Rhone-Alps region also likes chocolate. Just like its Swiss neighbour, it mixes it with local products, from milk to hazel nuts. Establishments such as Cémoi, in Grenoble, have made their world-wide reputation from it. But there are also excellent cho-colate-makers in Saint-Étienne (Weisse) and in Lyon: the most well-known masters in the conglomeration include Bernachon (Maurice and Jean-Jacques), Voisin, Ginet and Paillasson. In any event, one takes great delight in cocons, coussins, chardons, palets d'or, bâtons de Guignol and other delights from the Beaujolais region.

Little dry cakes have for a long time been symbolised by Grenoble's Brun biscuits. The Pérouges gridle cake, very delicate and sweet, made like a Romans brioche, a large brioche with praline. And children always love apple turnovers.

There is a wide variety of fruit. The Rhone Valley begins at Lyon and orchards abound in the south-west part of the conglomeration, starting from Irigny: apple-trees (half of which produce the Golden variety), pear-trees (ahh! Beaujolais-style pears...), peach-trees (one third of the French production is produced in the Rhone-Alps region), apricot trees (40% of French production), to which are added the cherry-trees found throu-ghout the region, especially along the Brévenne valley (Bessenay whiteheart cherries). In winter, one can add to this list the Ardèche chestnuts (alternately, marrons and châtaignes in French) and walnuts from Grenoble. There is nothing surprising that several popular fairs and festivals are held in the Lyon region and that the Teisseire syrups headquarters is located in the Dauphiné.

For unrepentant gourmands, there are such specialities as dame Fanny pancakes - those eaten by the bowls players - with rose hips jam (otherwise known as wild rosebush or dog rose, which supplies itching powder). Let nostalgia-ridden dreamers pace the ancient alleys in search of acacia flowers to perfume their fritters!

Translator's note: See syntax of original French text for this sentence ("The Pérouges girdle cake...")

Page 57. Apple tart from the small «Bouchon» Chez Georges and Lyon's famous Bugnes.

Bugnes : les roussettes

Bugnes

250g of flour, 25g of sugar,
100g of butter,
2 eggs, 1 glass of rum,
1 pinch of salt.

- Pour the flour out on the table, make a hollow in the centre, add the sugar, the softened butter, the salt, the 2 beaten eggs and the glass of rum.
- Knead the paste until it no longer sticks to your hands.
- Leave the paste to rest for at least two hours.
- Roll the paste out into a thin layer.
- Cut the paste into strips and shapes with a pastry wheel.
- Fry in oil at 180°C and turn the bugne over when it reaches a golden brown colour.
- Place the bugnes on some kitchen paper to absorb the oil then sprinkle plenty of icing sugar over them.

Tarte aux pommes

Apple tart

Ingredient :
4 Golden delicious apples
4 soup spoons of sugar
150 g of butter

Pastry :
250 of flour
1 whole egg
1 spoonful of sugar
1/2 of water and milk
- Roll the pastry into a thin layer.
- Lay the pastry on a tart dish (don't forget to prick it with a fork).
- Cut the apples into thin slices. Arrange the slices tightly against each other in a spiral starting from the outer side of the tart dish.
- Sprinkle with sugar, add knobs of butter and bake to a golden brown in a medium hot oven for about 45 minutes.
- Turn the tart out of the tart dish as soon as you take it out of the oven.
- Serve hot or cold.

C'est à boire qu'il nous faut

What we need is something to drink

Vineyards are everywhere and although today, one no longer drinks wine either from Guillotière or from Sainte-Foy (-lès-Lyon), Lyon vineyards are added to the Beaujolais and to the Côtes-du-Rhone vineyards; it is significant that the latter sell two-thirds of their production in western Europe, thus establishing a permanent link with Lyon-style and regional cooking. Nonetheless, one should not forget the wines of Savoie and Bugey or those of the Roanne Cotes and Forez, the Vivarais or Auvergne - and this is not to mention all the old lesser-known wines of regions which are now disappearing. Sparkling wines, preferred by some as aperitifs or as dessert wines, are not lacking either, from cerdon and seyssel to the light sparkling wine of Die, not to mention montagnieu and saint-péray. The Lyon pot, a vestige of older units of measure before the revolutionary unification, is 46 centilitres - at least it has been since 1846, since, before that, it reached 1.04 litres - in thick glass; recently it has been given its pride of place by Beaujolais producers, but in the standardised appearance of 50 centilitres and quite thinned down.

On this matter, one should not forget that the New Beaujolais is a recent commercial success, literally destined to immerse France and the rest of the world with a wine which is pleasant, it is true, but which is not to be compared with the ten vintages which have been left longer to age, even if only for several months. Moreover, the primeur fashion has spread to Côtes-du-Rhone and to Coteaux-du-Lyonnais. If, in Lyon, some people claim to like only wine from Bordeaux, no one can deny the wide diversity of regional wines, from the northerly Côtes-du-Rhone (côte-rôtie, condrieu) up to the southern Burgundies which are, to be sure, Beaujolais wines, such as saint-amour, juliénas and moulin-à-vent (which, nonetheless, are not, as wrote Gabriel Chevallier in Clochemerle, «a simple comet's tail»).

As an aperitif, the kir - also known as a blanc-cassis (white wine and blackcurrant) - and, to a lesser degree, its red-wine version called the communard, have become very commonplace, banishing wines made from oranges, walnuts or peaches as well as gentiane. After-dinner drinks may be made both with Bugey marc as well as with Chasselay pear eau-de-vie, guignolet from the Dauphiné and verveine from Velay or génépi from the Alps, or even arquebuse or chartreuse. Nor should one forget that alcohol is used in sauces (such as vigneronne), from coq au vin to eel fish stew, including eggs in meurette (an old, medieval recipe), andouillettes with white wine, and sausage with red wine.

Andouillette beaujolaise

Andouillette Beaujolaise

- Cook the andouillette in a frying pan with some shallots without browning them.
- Add salt, pepper and allspice.
- Baste with Beaujolais wine, let the wine boil down then add a little more wine.
- Serve.

Restaurant La Bressane
Recipe by Jean-Pierre Duplouy
2, rue de Cuire - 69004 Lyon

Beignets d'acacia

Acacia fritters

For 3 people.
125 g of flour
1 egg
1 pinch of salt
2 spoonfuls of melted butter
10 cl of beer, 10 cl of water
300 g of acacia flowers
150 g of sugar
White rum.

- Mix the flour, the egg, the salt, the butter, the beer and the water together.
- Leave to rest on a radiator.
- After washing the acacia flowers and removing their stalks, sprinkle the sugar on them, then the white rum.
- Leave to macerate for 2 hours.
- Beat the egg white until stiff then incorporate the fritter mixture.
- Dip the flowers in the batter and shake off any excess.
- Fry a spoonful at a time.
- Drain off the fat and sprinkle with sugar.
- Serve hot.

Page 61. The omnipresent Beaujolais and andouillette in Beaujolais, restaurant La Bressane.

Se forcer

Forcing oneself

Édouard Herriot, whose table was famous and who, as we have seen, knew the folk origin of food from his city, humorously exclaimed, *«On the job, one does what one can, but when one sits down to the table, one forces oneself!»* This is doubtless the reason why he was a little «broadened out», he on whom his entourage tried to force restraint.

Beyond this invitation to the courage of the Epicurean, there is the question of the future of this style of preparing meals. For several reasons: first of all, the proliferation of the fast-food establishments, which have replaced the old brasseries, and pizzerias which make home-deliveries, and which compete with caterers; then, new customs, which have resulted in substantial changes in tastes and manners (Michel Noir replaced meals in splendid back rooms and private dining rooms with sober meals, quickly prepared); finally, the oversimplification of our period, which retains only a few terms, often misused in the cheaper restaurants in Old Lyon. In fact, although the city and region have been able to resist the nouvelle cuisine to a great extent, the better restaurants have suffered substantially in the economic crisis of the 1990's; whatever the ultimate reasons may be, the Mère Guy, the Gourmandin, Bourillot and Vettard, to mention only a few of the most well-known, have disappeared.

But one cannot end on a pessimistic note. Through the persistence of strong deep-seated regional traditions and intelligence - involving both culinary and commercial aspects - of its chefs, Lyon is still the symbol of good living, accessible to the masses and worthy of a reputation going back to the Roman emperors and Rabelais.

Bibliography

Androuët (Pierre), *L'almanach des fromages*, Éditions Atlas, Paris, 1985, sans pagination [en fait, 32 pages]

Benoit (Félix), *La cuisine des traboules*, Solar, Paris, 1983, 244 pages

Benoit (Félix), *La cuisine lyonnaise*, Solar, Paris, 1987, 284 pages [une première édition était sortie en 1972 en collaboration avec Henry Clos-Jouve]

Bocuse à la carte, avec le concours d'Yvonne de Blaunac, Flammarion, Paris, 1986, 88 pages

Bocuse (Paul), *Bon appétit !*, Flammarion, Paris, 1989, 200 pages

Bocuse (Paul), *Cuisine de France*, avec la collaboration de Martine Albertin et Anne Grandclément assistées de Pascale Couderc, Flammarion, Paris, 1990, 256 pages

Bonniel (Jacques), *Lyon capitale mondiale de la gastronomie*, in *Lyonnais-Beaujolais*, Editions Bonneton, Paris, 1991, 432 pages

Bourgeois (Louis), *Le Rhône*, in *Pays et gens du Rhône*, Larousse/Sélection du Reader's Digest, Paris, 1983, 120 pages

Bourillot (Christian), *Cuisinier à Lyon*, Renaudot et Cie, Paris, 1989, 272 pages

Bourin (Jeanne), *Cuisine médiévale pour table d'aujourd'hui*, Flammarion, Paris, 1983 [réédition en 1995], 256 pages

Casati-Brochier (François), *La «Gastronomie» de Berchoux et la région lyonnaise*, Editions Bellier, Lyon, 1994, 192 pages

Chauvy (Gérard), *Lyon*, La Taillanderie, Bourg-en-Bresse, 1990, 168 pages

Chevallier (Gabriel), *Clochemerle*, Éditions Rombaldi, Paris, 1976, 440 pages [édition originale chez Rieder en 1934]

Couderc (Philippe), *Les plats qui ont fait la France*, Julliard, Paris, 1995, 288 pages

Cuisine (La) des bouchons lyonnais, À l'enseigne du porte-pot, Bourg-en-Bresse [?], 1991, 240 pages

Curnonsky [Edmond Sailland, dit], *Cuisines et vins de France*, Larousse, Paris, 1987, 704 pages [en fait, une refonte contemporaine]

Decraene (Jean-François), *Le tour de France par un gourmand*, Horvath, Lyon, 1995, 480 pages

Devos (Marie-Agnès) et Gambier (Gérald), *Saveurs du pays de Brillat-Savarin*, La Taillanderie, Bourg-en-Bresse, 1995, 168 pages

Dictionnaire d'Amboise Lyonnais, Editions d'Amboise, Chambéry, 1990, 432 pages

Ducloux (Jean) et ses collaborateurs, *La cuisine traditionnelle*, Solar, Paris, 1987 [réédition en 1994], 120 pages

Dufourt (Jean), *Calixte ou l'introduction à la vie lyonnaise*, Plon, Paris, 1926 [réédition en 1978], 192 pages

Fontaine (Jacques), *Recettes et cuisines d'autrefois*, Horvath, Lyon, réimpression de 1995, 144 pages

Fontaine (Jacques), *La gastronomie*, in Pelletier (André) [sous la direction d'], *Le guide du Rhône*, Horvath, Lyon, 1992, 176 pages

Fromages (Les) en Rhône-Alpes, dossier de presse, CPM, Lyon, s.d. [en fait, 1992], 14 feuilles

Gardes (Gilbert), *Le voyage de Lyon*, Horvath, Lyon, 1993, 390 pages

Garrier (Gilbert), *Les vins et la table*, in *Rhône-Alpes*, Hachette-Guides bleus, Paris, 1991, p. 115-122

Gilbert (François) et Gaillard (Philippe), *Les vins de Savoie*, Solar, 1991, 96 pages

Grison (Pierre), *Les meilleures tables de Rhône-Alpes*, Compagnie lyonnaise de média, Lyon, 1988, 112 pages

Grison (Pierre) et Bay (Agathe), *Nouvelles merveilles de la cuisine lyonnaise*, Editions Xavier Lejeune, Lyon, 1996, 144 pages

Grison (Pierre) et Benoit (Félix), *Gastromiam lyonnais*, Éditions du Signe noir, Lyon, 1982, 120 pages

Grison (Pierre) et Godet (Michel), *Les merveilles de la cuisine lyonnaise*, Éditions Xavier Lejeune, Lyon, 1988, 144 pages

Grison (Pierre) et Lecoq (Philippe), *Les bouchons d'hier et d'aujourd'hui*, Le Progrès, Chassieu, 1994, 176 pages

Hermann (Marie-Thérèse), *La cuisine paysanne de Savoie*, La Fontaine de Siloé, Montmélian, 1994, 256 pages

Hugo (Abel), Verne (Jules) et Joanne (Adolphe), *Le Rhône*, Les Éditions du Bastion, s.l., 1990, 144 pages

Lallemand (Roger), *Les Savoies gastronomiques*, Éditions Charles Corlet, Condé-sur-Noireau, 1988, 180 pages

Lequin (Yves) [sous la direction de], *Rhône-Alpes 500 années lumière. Mémoire industrielle*, Plon, Paris, 1991, 512 pages

Livre (Le) du chocolat, Flammarion, Paris, 1995, 216 pages

Mère Courtin, *La cuisine traditionnelle lyonnaise*, Éditions des Traboules, Brignais, 1991, 160 pages

Mérindol (Pierre), *Lyon. Les passerelles du temps*, La Taillanderie, Bourg-en-Bresse, 1988, 168 pages

Miège (Madeleine), *Le français de Lyon*, Pierre Masson, Lyon, 1937, réédité chez Jeanne Laffitte, Marseille, 1981, 2 + XII + 126 pages

Moreau (Roger), *Les secrets de la Mère Brazier*, Solar, Paris, 1992, 318 pages

Moreau (Roger), *La gastronomie*, in Pelletier (André) [sous la direction d'], *Grande encyclopédie de Lyon et des communes du Rhône*, Horvath, Roanne, t. II, 1981, p. 407-415

Puitspelu (Nizier du) [Tisseur (Clair), dit], *Le Littré de la Grand'Côte*, Storck, Lyon, 1894, réédité chez Jean Honoré, Lyon, 1980, 6 + 354 pages

Rhône-Alpes, l'encyclopédie, Musnier-Gilbert Éditions, Bourg-en-Bresse, 1993, 864 pages + 8 pages volantes d'addenda

Varille (Mathieu), *La cuisine lyonnaise*, Masson, Lyon, 1928, réédité chez Champion-Slatkine, Paris/Genève, 1987, 12 + 138 pages

Vurpas (Anne-Marie), *Le parler lyonnais*, Rivages, Paris, 1993, 296 pages

Werner (François), *Gastronomie lyonnaise*, in Bertin (Dominique) et Clémençon (Anne-Sophie), *Lyon*, Guide Arthaud, Paris, 1990, p. 35-40

Werner (François), *Grandes cuisines Rhône-Alpes*, Glénat, Grenoble, 1985, 128 pages

Achevé d'imprimer juin 1996
Dépôt légal 2e trimestre 1996
IMPRIME EN UE